HEARTS
—OF—
GOLD
BROKEN BODIES

KATHY POUNDS GRAHAM

CITI OF
BOOKS

CITIOFBOOKS, INC.
3736 Eubank NE Suite A1
Albuquerque, NM 87111-3579
www.citiofbooks.com
Hotline: 1 (877) 389-2759
Fax: 1 (505) 930-7244

Ordering Information:
Quantity sales. Special discounts are available on quantity purchases by corporations, associations, and others. For details, contact the publisher at the address above.

Printed in the United States of America.
ISBN-13:   Paperback   979-8-89391-748-2
                eBook   979-8-89391-750-5
                Hardback   979-8-89391-749-9

Library of Congress Control Number: 2025912147

TABLE OF CONTENT

ACKNOWLEDGEMENTS

Helene (Laney) Lindsey

Tammie Brown

Tammy Hoggle

Bill Harvison

Mark Covington

Vicki Killingsworth

Anita Scott

Marian Allen

Daniel L. and Valerie Buchanan

Special Mentions

Grandparents:

Maternal:

Troy W. Pounds and Ellen Louise Stanley
Pounds Bonds

Paternal:

James Odle and Mary Helen Parvin Odle

Beloved Nurse:

Helen Butler

HONORABLE MENTIONS:

Governor Ray Mabus

Sam Valentine MSDH Children's Program

Presley Posey

Association for the Care of Children's Health (ACCH)

US Department of Health and Human Services Maternal and Child Health

U S Surgeon General's Office Dr C. Everett Koop

Mississippi Department of Education

Mississippi State Department of Health Children's Medical Program

Mississippi Department of Vocational Rehabilitation

Brandi's Hope

Mississippi Department of Mental Health

INTRODUCTION

As I begin this book, I proudly introduce my two sons, Shawn and Jason Odle, as they become teenagers so full of love and excitement to challenge everything around them regardless of their limitations. You see they've never been told they aren't able to do that. Their minds always freely figure out their own way of overcoming obstacles.

A child should never be told they can't achieve something even though as adults we can't see all the possibilities.

This book is filled with stories of their adaptive thinking and personalities. As you read, my hope is you will gain the knowledge of unlimited possibilities.

CHAPTER ONE
SEASON OF CHANGE

In 1984 I was invited to the annual Association for the Care of Children's Health (ACCH) conference in San Francisco. This would be the beginning of our journey into national advocacy. Many contacts were made and a wonderful group of fellow parents of children with special needs. As involvement grew, opportunities surfaced.

In May 1985 we were invited to present at the ACCH conference in Halifax, Nova Scotia, Canada. This was an adventure for several of us as we decided to make it and educational trip as well. Three other parents with their children made the trip in a 33-foot motor home from northeast Mississippi to Halifax Nova Scotia. The trip had many planned educational stops. Traveling to Canada we stopped at the Natural Bridge in Virginia. In New York we visited the Statue of Liberty. I'll forever remember Jason saying She's green!!! He'd only seen it in pictures.

As we entered Canada we viewed Prince William Sound. Returning we made stops in <u>Boston Massachusetts</u>

Washington DC

Our visit was brief as we had to completed our trip home. Many sites were unvisited with plans to for another visit.

Happy Place SC

It was an amazing and peaceful place to experience. God's presence was certainly there.

We watched a video of astronauts floating freely in space. Shawn and Jason were amazed at the idea of floating free of gravity. I could only imagine their thoughts of freedom. They had difficulty with abstract thinking. Everything was simple thinking with them.

In 1986 I was invited to present at the annual ACCH conference in Anaheim CA.

In May of 1986 we were invited to Washington DC by C, Everett Koop, Surgeon General, to testify regarding the benefits of early intervention to children with disabilities. We had been picked because the early services which my guys received were community based and beneficial to their health and development. Their providers were invited as our team to testify. The team included their pediatrician, their teacher and their after-school provider. This would set the stage for farther advocacy. You see, even when a federal law or mandate is passed, the states still must choose to implement the program.

In the spring of 1987, we attended the governor's signing of the Early Intervention Act in Mississippi. I shall never forget that day Jason decided to go down steps in his wheelchair even though he had been shown numerous times why he shouldn't. A ramp for wheelchairs was visible only a few feet away. He caught me with my back turned helping Shawn. Imagine my horror seeing this 300-pound plus wheelchair on top of my baby boy. He was unconscious!! My fears and mind went into overdrive. Capitol EMS was called and responded quickly. I had already wedged my legs underneath his wheelchair to take the weight off him. As they raised the wheelchair up with him buckled in it his eyes opened. My heart leaped but my fears never left. As he was taken to the local hospital emergency room my mind was overthinking. The sweetest sound to my ears came when I entered the emergency room and heard laughter. Not just his laughter but the entire staff plus the blessed paramedics. His only injury was a goose size bump on his forehead. No concussion. No broken bones. He was saying 'I did it!' My little Evel Knievel!! Never again did I turn my back on him.

For the next month everyone would look

at me as if I'd abused him with both his eyes blackened!! Shawn was always the careful one. Studying a situation as well as people before engaging. Not Jason!!! The only way to assure Jason's safety when we were not watching him was to disengage the motor to his wheelchair. Of course, we always engaged him in what we were doing. They were typical teenagers in every way. Their personalities were totally opposites, which made me grow as a human being and a mother.

Many ask about their daddy. Some subjects are difficult to speak of and best left alone. Such is the topic of my marriage to Shawn and Jason's daddy. I will briefly address the topic here as it is the reason for this change. After 15 years of marriage through my struggles and issues along with filing for divorce twice, I gave up on my marriage. The divorce was final on December 11, 1987, but the struggles weren't over. The obsessive jealousy and stalking became worse along with him turning family and friends against me. After carefully studying the circumstances and my son's future, I know I could not stay any longer. I began praying fervently for a solution.

My sons were always involved with the

Gumtree Festival in Tupelo every year. This year 1988 was a political year. Many politicians were present. Among them was Ray Mabus who was running for Governor. We had already been formally introduced during some advocacy events as he was serving as the Secretary of State. As he and I were talking, Jason wanted some of the attention!! His grinning and interrupting weren't getting it!! He literally rolled his powered wheelchair between Ray and me, stopping it right on top of Ray's foot!! Oh my!! If anyone knows those chairs are heavy!! I scolded him and apologized to Ray while Jason was smirking. Amazingly Ray turned his positive attention to my guys, which was a delight for all involved.

In February of 1989 I was appointed to his staff as an advisor on the development of early intervention services in our state for children with or at risk of disabilities. We made our move to Jackson, Mississippi and into an unsuspecting world of social challenges.

With recognition as spokes persons for disability and change, many opportunities became available.

The schools were more advanced in the area of inclusion with appropriate age peers. Shawn attended Pearl High School from which he graduated, and Jason attended Pearl Middle School. After school they went to the Boy's Club of Pearl.

Recreation consisted of weekends with outing with the Outreach Christian Program and Challenger League Baseball. The joy of seeing them play baseball was beyond description. They loved watching sports and enjoyed seeing the excitement in the action. For them to be able to actually feel the action within their bodies and souls was so fulfilling for them as well as all of us.

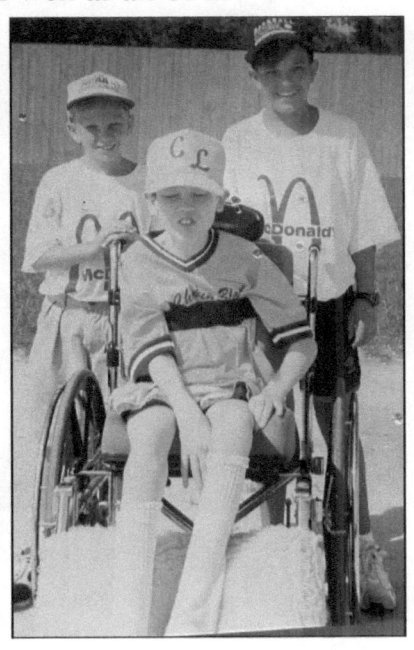

Jason and Shawn enjoyed their helpmates in the Challenger League. They helped him hit the ball and roll from base to base to make a home run. These young men were an absolute pleasure and gave all of us lasting memories. Wherever they are today in the grown-up world we wish to say Thank you and God bless y'all.

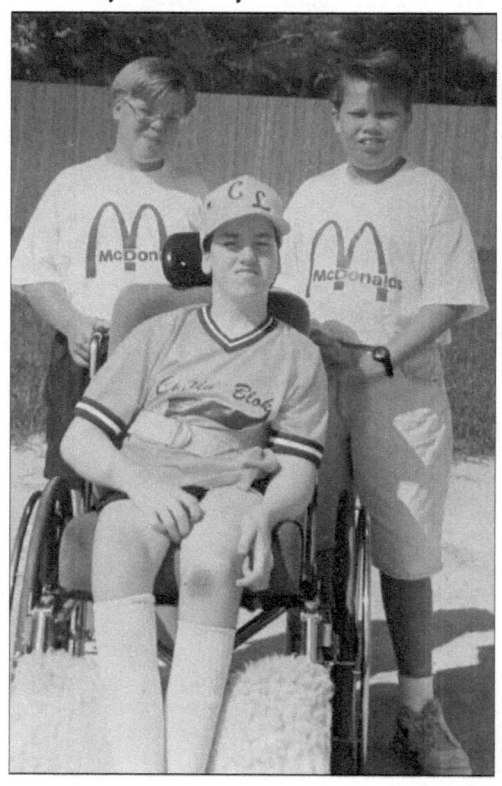

Challenger League Baseball Team

Chunky Cheese was their favorite place to go for fun and food.

The neighborhood Louisa Street in Pearl Mississippi which we moved into was a very close-knit group of very welcoming friendly people. Rusty Graham was our neighbor. He was very helpful in introducing us to the neighborhood. He worked for Shell Oil Company and was a musician. Weekends were always busy with recreation and entertainment.

When we first moved to Pearl, Mississippi not only my sons but I myself were introduced to the ice cream truck. Living in the country we never thought of such a thing. It was one of the highlights of the week. The only problem was we never knew exactly when he would come down our street. Getting two boys in wheelchairs to the street curb in time was a task!!! Soon the entire neighborhood was involved in keeping a watch for the ice cream truck. Eventually the driver made sure he drove very slowly on Louisa Street even stopping in front of our house. Rusty lived just across the street, and he'd detain the ice cream truck when necessary. Before long, our address became the place to meet the ice cream truck. This brought much delight and many friendships.

This was the true definition of 'It takes a village'.

Living on Louisa Street had many positive benefits, we had a routine of going to McDonald's for milkshakes and hamburgers <u>on Friday afternoon</u>. One Friday I had gotten busy and was late taking them. Jason decided he had waited long enough!! He left the house and took a right on Louisa Street in his motorized wheelchair. McDonald's was only 4 blocks away. Shawn never said a word but didn't join him. I was totally unaware until a neighbor at the end of the street we called Pawpaw came to the door with Jason beside him!! He asked 'are you missing a boy' as he proceeded with the story. He was raking in his yard when he saw Jason cruising down the street. He asked, 'Where are you going?' Of course, the answer was McDonald's. Thank God for Pawpaw. That afternoon Rusty put a chained gate up at the driveway to keep Houdini Jason safe. We could never underestimate his talents.

Shawn's shenanigans:

BEAVIS AND BUTTHEAD STORY

There was a monitoring system in our home in Pearl, MS. It was mainly for monitoring for their safety not to intrude upon their privacy. However, one day I had crossed the street to visit Rusty and had the monitors on. I tried to be careful of the television shows they watched. They had full use of their remote controls. Next thing I hear is Jason telling Shawn 'Mom don't like us watching Beavis and Butthead.'

Conversation followed. Shawn 'but Mom's not here.' I was about to go back across the street when Rusty stopped me and said, 'Just listen to them and you'll learn something.'

We listened and laughed. When I returned to the house I didn't say a word. Opportunity for conversation provided itself the next day when Jason could no longer contain the secret. I asked Shawn if he thought those guys behaved properly and used good language. Our agreement was Beavis and Butthead was a good learning of how not to behave. Watching it was okay as long as he didn't start acting like them. Issue solved. And he never did. Shawn was my thinker. He loved people and enjoyed studying them. He was a very quiet young man.

First Christmas in Pearl Mississippi near the capital of Jackson. 1989

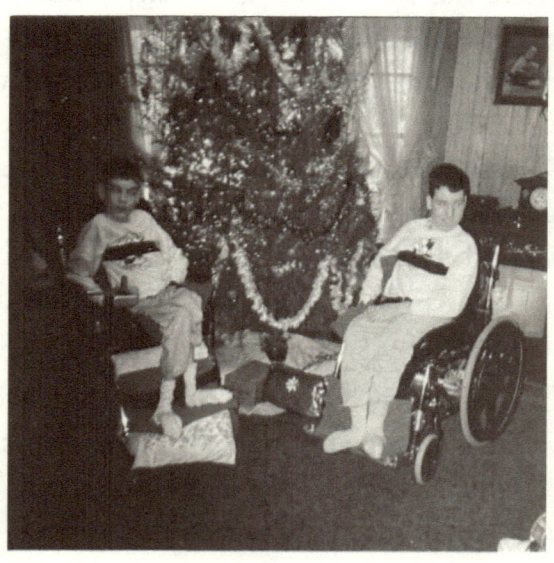

CLARION LEDGER NEWS Article 1989-1990 Working for the governor's office was a bit of a challenge because I was very outspoken especially when it came to my sons. I have searched for an article to share with all of you.

Many health challenges were encountered.

Shawn had pneumonia after being hospitalized. The doctor's warning was that pneumonia would be the greatest threat to my guys.

Later Shawn broke his leg at school as he was negotiating on the sidewalk. In life, accidents happen to our children. No panic!! No blaming!! Only time for action to ensure the lesson is learned not just for everyone around him but for himself. That lesson in life was to always pay attention to where you are going. Distractions happen and accidents happen. We see it happening every day in the world around us.

Jason was the more fragile one with health. At 17 years of age, he had difficulty chewing and swallowing his food. He began losing weight. Several changes were made which included blending his food, adding supplemental nutritional drinks and 5 small meals daily.

Nothing seemed to make a difference. A gastroenterologist was treating him. Later one evening he appeared to be going into a seizure which had never happened. He had to be sure someone was with Shawn as I rushed Jason to the emergency room. Rushing to the hospital only resulted in being sent home with an appointment with his neurologist the next day. As I watched my baby boy tremble and suffer, I became more afraid. I prayed for God does not mean for us to fear but to believe in Him. The next day was met with more frustration as he no longer had the strength to sit in his wheelchair. He was placed on a stretcher at the hospital clinic as we waited to see the neurologist, which only resulted in another appointment being scheduled several days away with the gastroenterologist. That clinic was just down the hall in the hospital!!! My baby was suffering. Time was being wasted!!! As the stretcher was being pushed to exit, we passed the gastroenterology clinic. No More!!! I took control and stopped the stretcher in front of the clinic door stating loudly "we aren't going anywhere until we see this doctor!! My baby is dying!!" Such a scene as caused that security was called. My response was "arrest me!! But please get the doctor for my son!!" Dr Parker heard me (God heard my plea). He stepped out and immediately had Jason taken into the clinic. Jason was immediately admitted, and tube feeding was started by nasal tube. He was in critical condition. The risk of aspiration became a danger

Jason became tube fed. Surgery was completed for permanent tube feeding.

San Antonio TX Surgeon General's Conference 1996 following Shawn's graduation and an all-night ride I presented the keynote speech.

We visited the Alamo afterwards. As my guys learned the history behind the site they began asking questions. All the why's couldn't be answered.

After Shawn graduated high school we moved to Waynesboro, MS with Rusty. He had a heart attack and was forced to retire. He asked if we would move with him as he made his home on a family farm.

This brought many changes as we participated in implementing the programs for which we had advocated.

CHAPTER 2
FROM ADVOCACY TO IMPLEMENTATION

Progress is slow in the advocacy for change. Getting laws and funding passed at the federal level doesn't ensure availability at the state and local levels. Even after the state's option in and implement the programs the quality of that service is not guaranteed. Advocacy is necessary at all levels. Too often policymakers and agency personnel have no idea how to implement programs in the community. This is the reason why there must be active participation by recipients of those services and their families at all levels. Having one involved in sitting at those conference tables discussing the implementation of services is vital. Sure, not everyone understands the process of program development, but you can bet we can tell you what will work and not work for our children and individual with a disability in our own communities. It takes both aspects to develop a clear vision of community implementation.

Summer of 1995, we moved to Waynesboro Mississippi. First challenge was the local school system. I was still the president of the Special

Education Committee with Mississippi State Board of Education Board. I tried to never use a position or title unless it was necessary to achieve purpose. I preferred to remain silent until the right moment.

Rusty (at that time) was a good friend and had gone to school with the special education coordinator. Piece of cake, right?!! WRONG!!! I listened politely through the meeting and while escorted through the isolated building called Shady Pines where students with severe disabilities were supposed to receive an education. When it came time to sign for the placement and the individualized educational plan I politely said Nope!! My sons (have) always been with (their) age-appropriate peers and I'll expect nothing less. At this point they were introduced to the fighting side of a determined mother. Later that afternoon upon returning home Rusty laughingly said his friend was flabbergasted asking him Why didn't you warn me who she was?!!! We both had a good laugh. The next day they tried sending Jason to Shady Pines first then planning his break and lunch with his peers. Well, here we go again!!!

To make a long story short Jason was placed in high school classes with an attendant with his appropriate age peers.

Parents' determination, knowledge and persistence is the key to getting what our students need.

He was settled in and included even in cheerleading for the football team

What bothered me most was thinking about those students I saw in that small little secluded building. One of the teachers there became a good friend. She would share stories with me without names. She told me when I came through the center, she knew Jason would not be coming there. I tried reaching out to parents in the area with little success. The state parent training group was useless. The advocacy group would do nothing without parental complaints. I only wondered how many other places accepted only the bare minimal and not much more than a baby-sitting service. Each child regardless of limitations has potential they can reach but only if they are challenged. Just like any student.

It was a rainy day, and I was stuck in the office work when I received a call from the high school principal. I could hear Jason in the background fussing. The school was only 3 blocks away, so I excused myself from work.

As I entered the school's visitor waiting area I could hear him. When he saw me, he calmed down. His teacher was patiently trying to approach him, and he'd have nothing to do with her. Upon inquiring I was told the teacher in geography, had been mentioning places on the map of the United States. Jason would say I've been there. In front of the entire class, she confronted him saying there's no way you've been to all these places. Oh boy!!! The fight was on!! He unconsolably started screaming and crying. I asked what places and as I confirmed yes, he's been there, he began to smile with that I told you do look!!! Apologies were made and Jason became a celebrity in the classroom. We shared pictures with the class of all his and his brother's adventures.

They were underestimated by many throughout their lifetime. They opened many people's eyes to their world.

Another such incident occurred with one of their nurses. There had been an electrical storm the night before. The tv was plugged into one of those sockets which can be turned on and off at the wall. Shawn had a good habit of turning every switch off when going to bed. Such he did that night. The next morning the nurse couldn't get the TV to come on. She called me at my office. After she explained the problem, I asked, "What are Shawn and Jason doing?' The reply answered it all as she said, 'oh they're just laughing not upset at all'. I took her through the regiment of flipping the wall switch on and then turned the TV on. Bingo!! Now what are they doing? She answered they are laughing at me! If only she had asked them they would've told her!!! Her attitude and respect for them changed very quickly. You see, they had to have assisted in doing almost everything but not because they didn't know it was a physical limitation.

New caregivers often fall victim to their humor.

So where was Shawn while Jason was finishing school!! He attended a work activity center. It was the first year they were separated during the day. Shawn was not happy. He protected his little brother. One day Jason had an accident going to the bus to come home. He was loaded anyway. No calls to me. He had a broken collarbone. 'Where was his attendant!' A meeting with the principal revealed Jason's attendant was busy doing a task assigned by a teacher. Jason, being independently minded, attempted to get on the bus by himself. He ran off the sidewalk. The attendant never left Jason alone after that. He's my little wild child. My daredevil which you can't turn your back on. He made life very interesting!!! Shawn was very upset. He was more upset than I was. He demanded that his brother be strictly guarded.

Shawn enjoyed the activities at the center. He learned many skills not taught at school. He learned crafts and many creative things. The center staff was very good at assisting him. He made several friends. One summer we assisted him

In planting a garden on hay bales. He loved his flowers and the butterflies.

Keeping good dependable caregivers was an ongoing issue. They'd start out good. We always called that the honeymoon phase. Next thing you know there'd be tardiness, forgetfulness or constant problems getting to work. We had just about every issue from stealing to neglect. The hardest part was my guys would become attached to them loving them and they'd take that for granted. Most never realized Shawn and Jason, although their speech was labored, they could very intelligently express their disappointments. This is often overlooked by caregivers. They don't take the time to listen. Communication is very vital for an individual who has limitations. It takes patience and a willingness to understand. Respect is very important.

Moving also required a change in employment, but I would still be a state employee working for the Institute of Disability Studies at the University of Southern Mississippi in Hattiesburg located approximately 66 miles southeast of Waynesboro. I worked there for 3 years when a job became available with the District Health Department which would allow me to be closer to home as Rusty was getting worse.

Beginning a job which was part of a system we had helped create was interesting. My first day with the First Steps Early Intervention Program was a bit disappointing. What was supposed to be a service in the community was laden with the unavailability of service providers. In rural areas services were nonexistent in the home. The struggle to get these services was left to the service coordinators with little support from the district office. The lack of providers such as physical, speech and occupational therapists was replaced with teachers in special education. Therapists were only brought in to consult or evaluate. The teachers were a blessing.

It was through this work experience that we met amazing children and mothers like.

Perryea Williams, child and Nichole, his mother. Shawn and Jason made friends with many of the children.

The love which was shared between our children drew all of us closer. Several others which I can't mention were amazing advocates for their children. The struggle was real for parents, service providers as well as the lead agency.

In order to provide management and oversight of Shawn and Jason's care and ensure they'd always have control over their lives ODLE was formed. This was not an organization nor advocacy group but a close-knit group of people with love and goal of making life the best it could be for them. As I was getting older, I had to know if I was gone there would be structured protection to ensure their rights to live and love as they had always done.

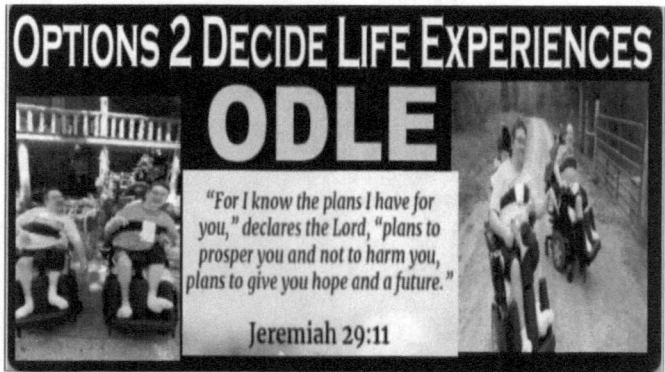

OPTIONS 2 DECIDE LIFE EXPERIENCES

ODLE

"For I know the plans I have for you," declares the Lord, "plans to prosper you and not to harm you, plans to give you hope and a future."

Jeremiah 29:11

There's so much involved in maintaining a safe productive environment in any life but especially when it involves others coming into your home as a part of that effort. The understanding of the entire purpose must be respected. That respect begins with the person, their needs, wishes and desires. As a parent

I was a part of this team not as a boss but a team player with the leading role for my sons. I couldn't do it alone. Each person was just as important as the next one, but no one was more important than Shawn and Jason. Everyone was respected. We knew each other as if we were family because we were. We cared for each other as we performed our tasks of taking care of 'our guys'. You see, they weren't just my sons. They were precious to everyone who came into their lives and became a part of their team. We were a family.

One of the hardest things to adjust with of home care was the ability to open your home to the daily presence of others coming and going performing duties which are necessary to keep and maintain their independence. There is little privacy without respect which must come from all parties involved. A steady routine of schedules is maintained for consistency. Each month a work schedule was presented to the staff for review and possible changes ending availability of the caregivers. Flexibility from everyone was necessary to maintain a steady flow of caregiving. We all respected and worked with one another to make everyone's life away from Shawn and Jason better. They loved to hear about their caregivers' families, often engaging in phone conversations with and meeting some of them. All I can say is 'The team provided more than caregiving. They provided love and an expended family of the most special kind.'

Keeping quality dependable caregivers wasn't easy. Many came and went but the ones who stayed were meant to be with us. It was easy to see how they blended with the goal and our family - God Sent. Shawn and Jason had the final say in hiring and firing their caregivers. Because of their severe limitations in mobility and speech some people weren't aware of how well they communicated their feelings. Their complaints were never overlooked and many failed their test. Being a caregiver isn't easy. It requires putting your ideas aside and fitting into another person's ideas about how they want things done. When hiring we always had a saying 'When you enter the gate, leave all your drama and personal ideas at the gate. They'll still be there when you leave for no one will steal them. '. Staff meetings were held as often as necessary. Some meetings were for discipline, but most were to discuss better ways of getting things done. We all grew together to provide the best possible outcomes for Shawn and Jason with them as priory, and I'm controlled.

I'll never forget the several times they've told me 'I fired __so and so.' They were never questioned but most of the time volunteered their reason. Majority of the time it was because of disrespect toward them. They loved, honored and respected and only asked for the same in return. Isn't that what we all want?!!

When I say I was a part of their team I don't mean just as their mom. I have filled in as a caregiver on numerous occasions when a worker wasn't available or a no show occurred. Just because my sons where adults with their own home did not mean my duties ended. They just took on a different role. You see I too had to respect their home, their independence and lifestyle. Just because I was Mom didn't mean I could take over!!!! Again RESPECT!!

Are there things I'd do differently looking back now. Maybe a few but very few. One of their longtime caregivers now lives with me. We sat and talk. Listening to her makes me study and see things deeper and at times differently. You will hear her story in her testimony ' To Know Me is To Love Me.'

Glorify Our Amazing Lord (GOAL) was formed after a futures planning meeting in which both young men expressed their interest in sharing God's Word. It's an online effort of sharing and carrying God's Word to the world. Ministers as well as those who believe in the Father, the Son and the Holy Spirit are welcomed to post, share and encourage one another as we share God's Word and do it best to walk in the footsteps of Jesus. We continue this effort in honor of Shawn and Jason and continue to glorify his Holy Name.

CHAPTER 3
MY SONS BECAME MEN

Moving to Waynesboro Mississippi brought about another initiative for people with disabilities. It was a program called Home of Your Own through the University of Southern Mississippi Institute for Disability Studies for whom I worked. Shawn and Jason were the first in the program in Mississippi to achieve buying their own home. We all participated in presentations along with the program coordinator Vicki Killingsworth who was an amazing woman who overcame many odds also.

Shawn senior prom date was his favorite neighbor. He was so proud she accepted. They were the best of friends.

Jason's Senior Prom 1998

Jason and his high school sweetheart
Maria at the Senior Prom.

Birthdays were always special. A time to celebrate. They still are special, and we still celebrate. Just differently now.

Balloons were released with each holding a
message inside of contact for Shawn.

Jason's birthday celebrations

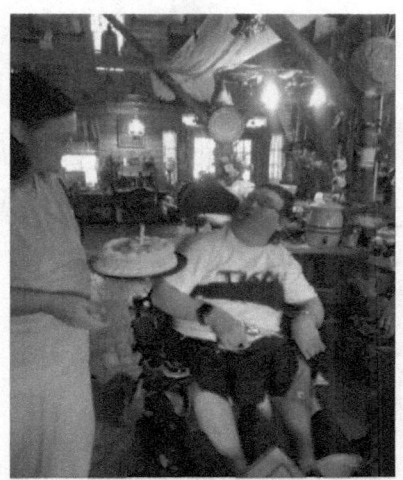

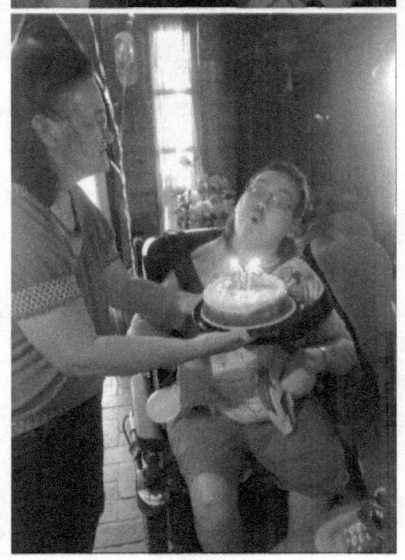

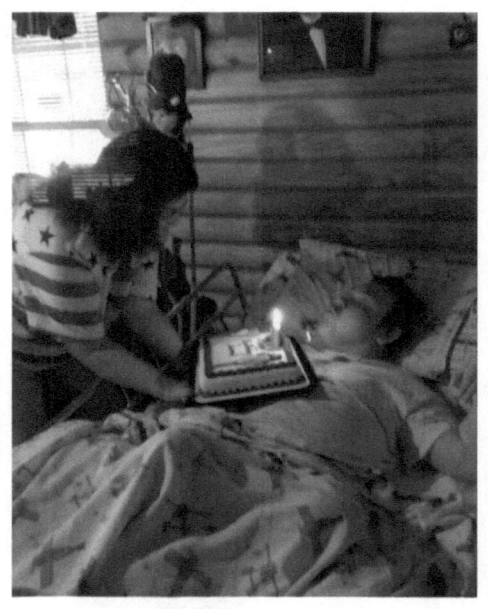

As years passed it seemed Jason would be sick
on his birthdays.

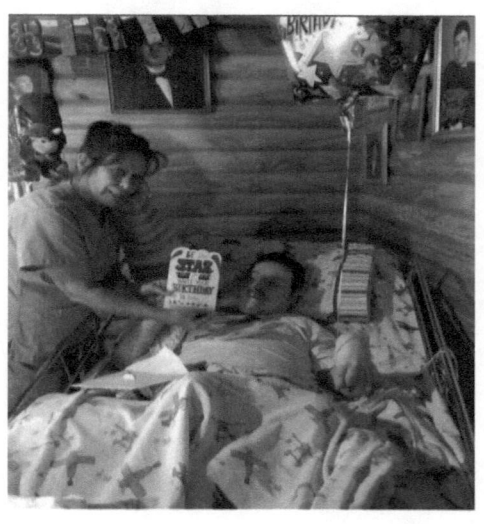

Shawn's birthdays continued

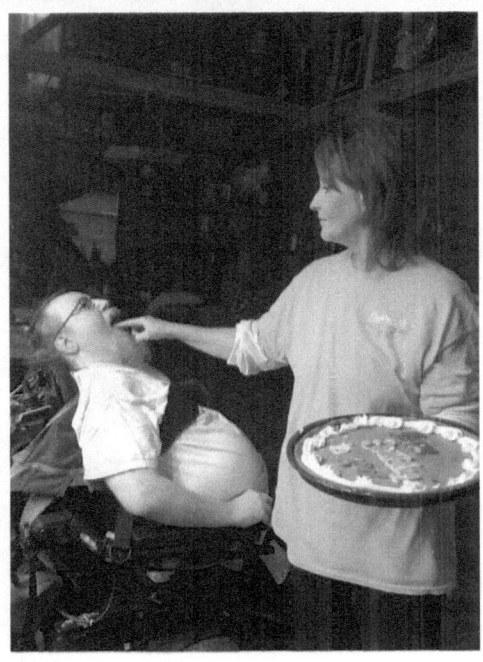

Christmas play

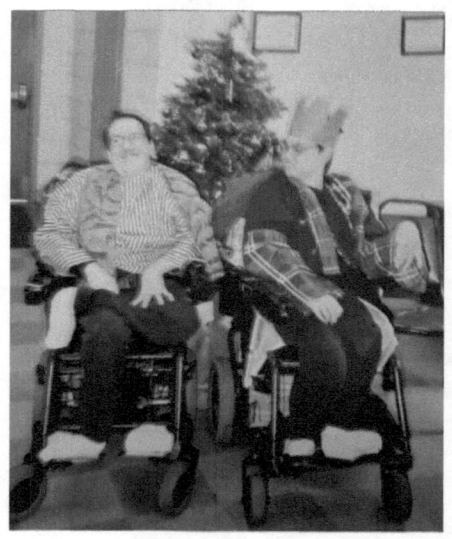

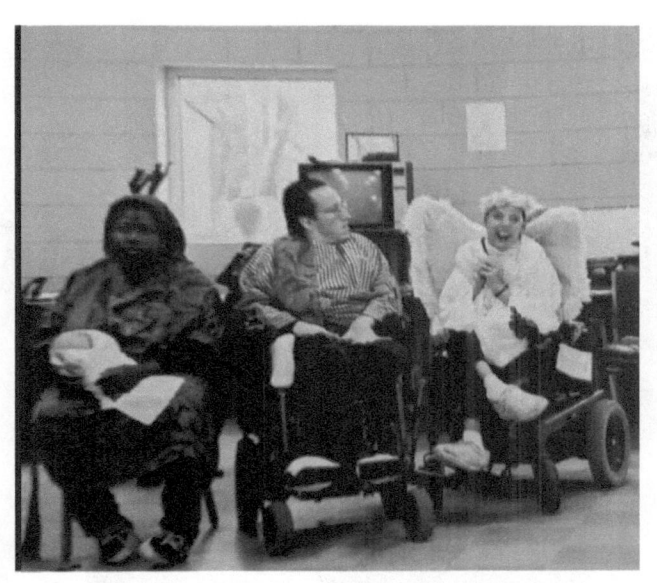

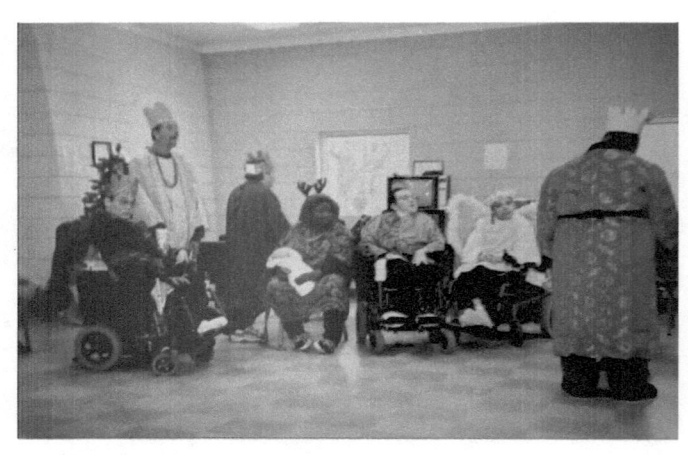

Halloween Party

Carving pumpkins!! Ooo!! Messy they said!!

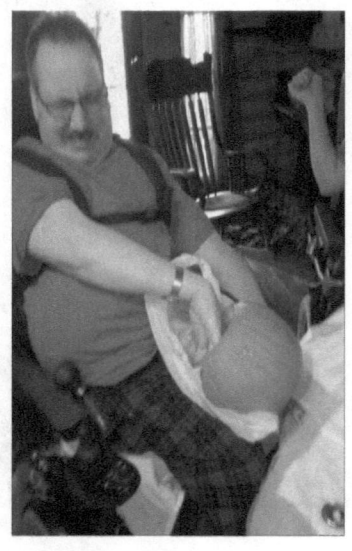

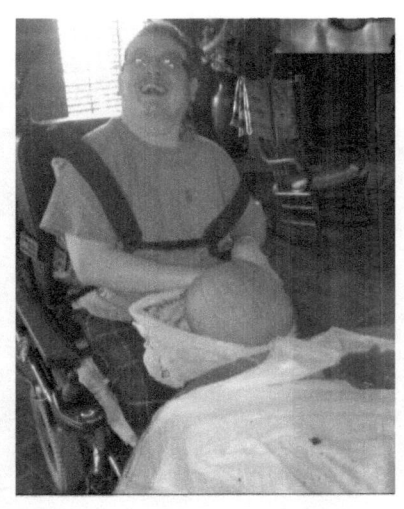

A big brother's love and protection.

Enjoying their pets and animals on the farm.
Visiting with Jax and horsing around.

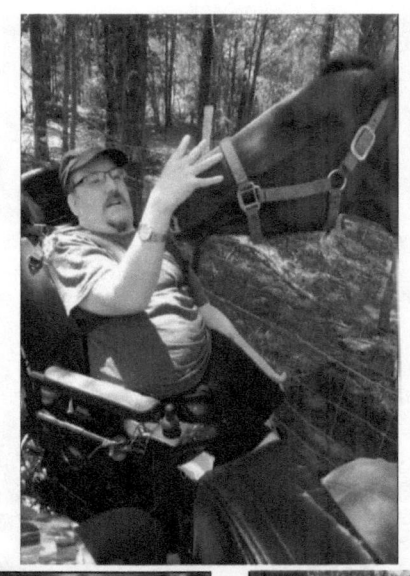

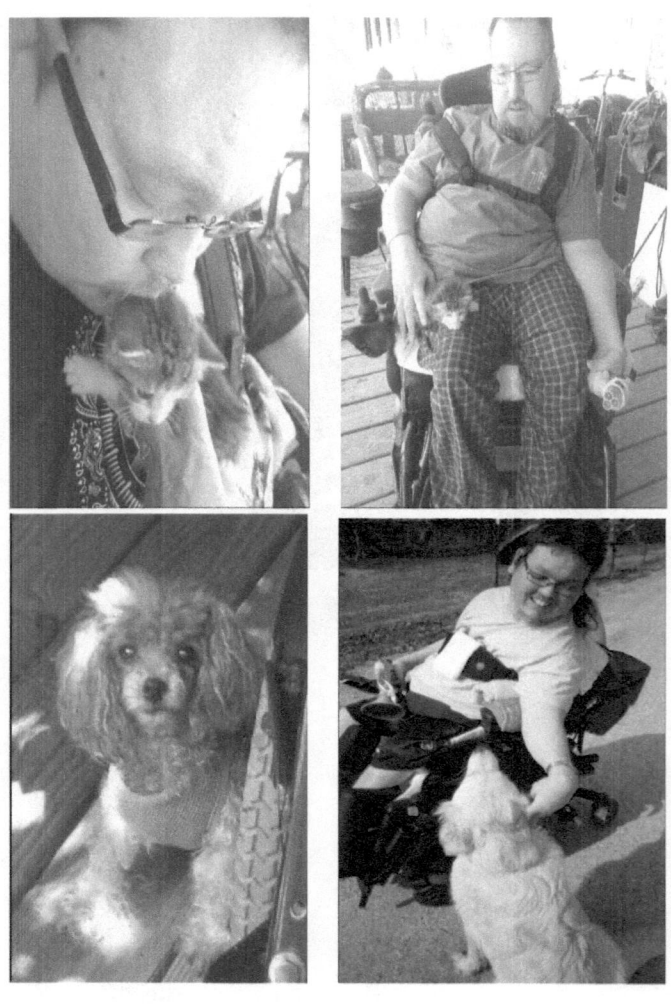

After they retired from the work activity center their joy was helping with the farm and the animals. They even volunteered for animal rescue.

They also enjoyed sharing and working on their online ministry GOAL (Glorify Our Amazing Lord). They enjoyed sharing and interacting with ministers and those who loved and believe in Jesus.

Valentine's Day

My guys!!! Thank you Helene Lindsey for assisting them. 🩶

Shawn's hello from Seldom Rest Farm as Jason and he took their daily stroll to check the goats and a visit to the front. They would sit in the driveway and wave at truckers who would blow their big horns for them.

Boxing gloves seem to be the perfect gift!! They were definitely typical brothers. They could get into arguments but nobody else bother them. Shawn loved to tease Jason. He would whisper things and Jason would scream out!! Shawn would look around so innocently.

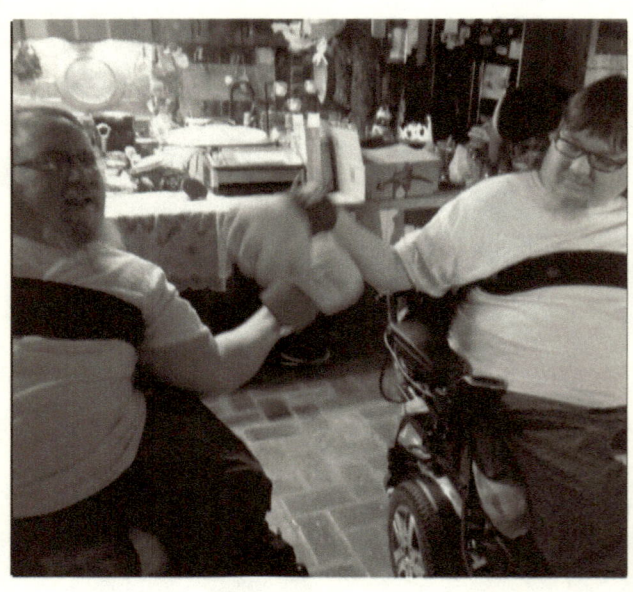

Psalms 23

1. The LORD is my shepherd; I shall not want.

2. He maketh me to lie down in green pastures: he leadeth me beside the still waters.

3. He restoreth my soul: he leadeth me in the paths of righteousness for his name's sake.

4. Yea, though I walk through the valley of the shadow of death, I willfear no evil: for thou art with me; thy rodand thy staff they comfort me.

5. Thou preparest a table before me in the presence of mine enemies: thou anointest my head with oil; my cuprunneth over.

6. Surely goodness and mercy shall follow me all the days of my life: and I will dwell in the house of the LORD forever.

The LORD is my Shepherd.

CHAPTER 4
BROTHERS' FINAL JOURNEY

This chapter is the hardest of all to write and share with the world. It's heart wrenching and soul bearing. It is the realization of how fragile our lives are and how important our relationship is with Jesus our Savior, God our Father and the Holy Spirit.

We had been very careful and didn't experience the effects of COVID in terms of illness. However, we were about to experience the cruel isolation from a loved one who would be suffering.

It all started July 7, 2021, at Wayne General Hospital with a young doctor's mistake. Jason's jugular vein and carotid artery were damaged when an IV port was attempted to be placed into his neck. After the profuse bleeding was slowed, he was immediately sent to South Central Regional Medical Center (SCRMC) 28 miles away. I was totally unaware of what had happened. I was not allowed into the ER room with him for the first time in our lives. At SCRMC he was intubated, and airlift was attempted but not available because of the weather. Jason was immediately placed in an ambulance with a registered nurse and rushed to University Medical Center in Jackson, Mississippi over 100 miles away. He was in critical condition. We followed behind the ambulance traveling at 100 plus miles per hour. It seemed to take an eternity. Repairing the damaged artery and vein couldn't be done until he was stabilized. That took 2 days. We were unable to stay with him. We could only see him for a few minutes 3 times a day.

To SCRMC in Laurel Mississippi

To UMC in Jackson Mississippi

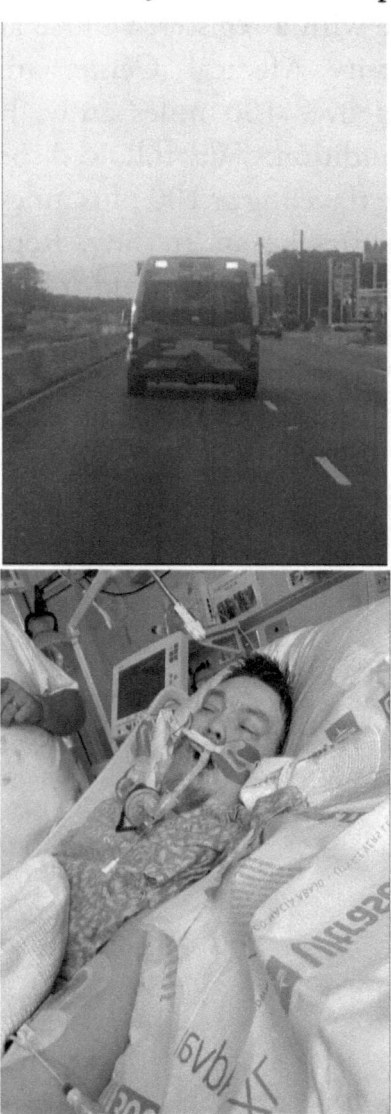

After surgical repair of the jugular vein and carotid artery he remained in a coma for 10 more days. We never stopped believing and praying. The room was darkened by the curtains. I requested that the sunlight be let into his room.

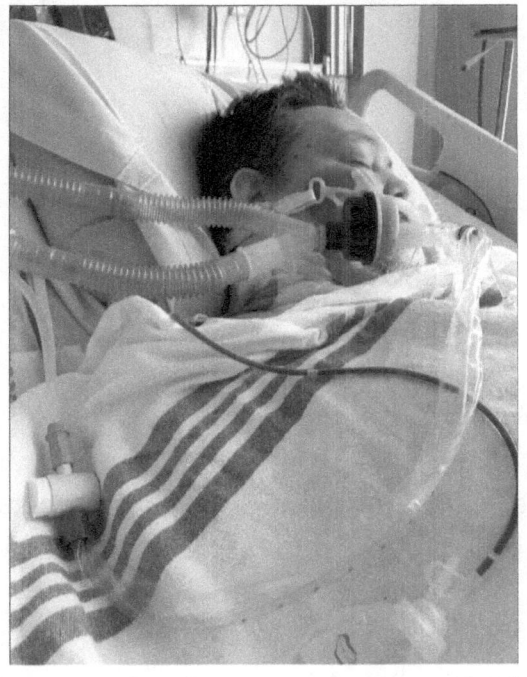

This was the first time the guys had been separated this long. It was taking a toll on all of us. The times I'd left Jackson to come home and spend time with Shawn left me worried and drained. Then leaving Shawn to go back to being with Jason felt so uncomfortable and I worried about Shawn.

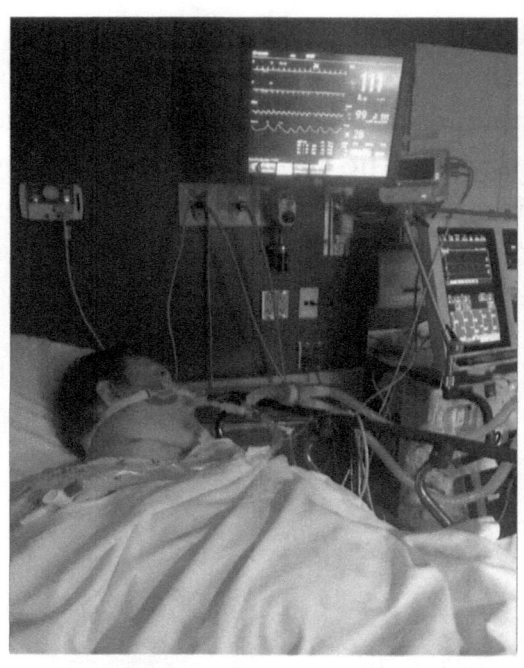

He opened his eyes and laughter and tears. No sound because he was intubated. What made him open his eyes was amazingly hilarious. Forgive me as I tell this. Previously there had been mention of a toy they each had. We called them Fart Guns. It was always amusing for them to pull the joke on someone. Well!!! A real one occurred. And I was talking to him. I asked, "Did you hear that Jaybird? His eyes came open as he started laughing. A ray of sunlight so beautiful and bright came through the window and showed on him. We all rejoiced. He was still heavily sedated and quickly went back unconscious but with his eyes open. It was quite frightening, but the nurse gently closed his eyes and placed a moist cloth on them. As the days passed and medication decreased, he became more interactive.

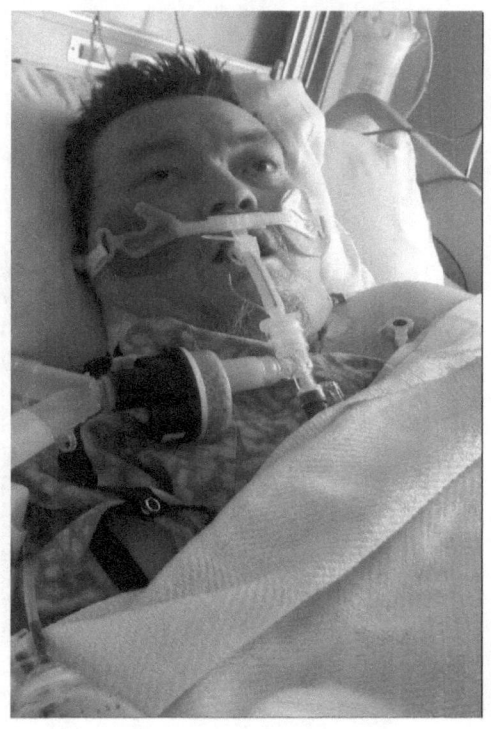

As Jason gained consciousness we would do FaceTime between them. It was hard for Shawn to see his little brother so sick and not with him. He was moved from Surgical ICU into a room, and I was able to stay 24/7 with him.

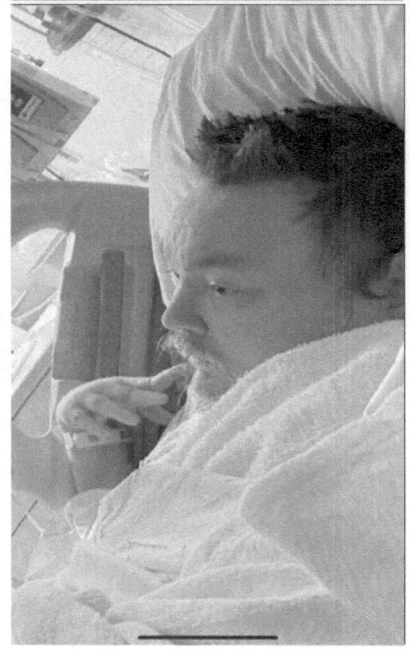

The nurses were wonderful. We finally were discharged 9/5/2021 with a follow up appointment for surgery to remove some kidney stones. His fever had ceased but we were warned the sepsis could return due to his kidneys.

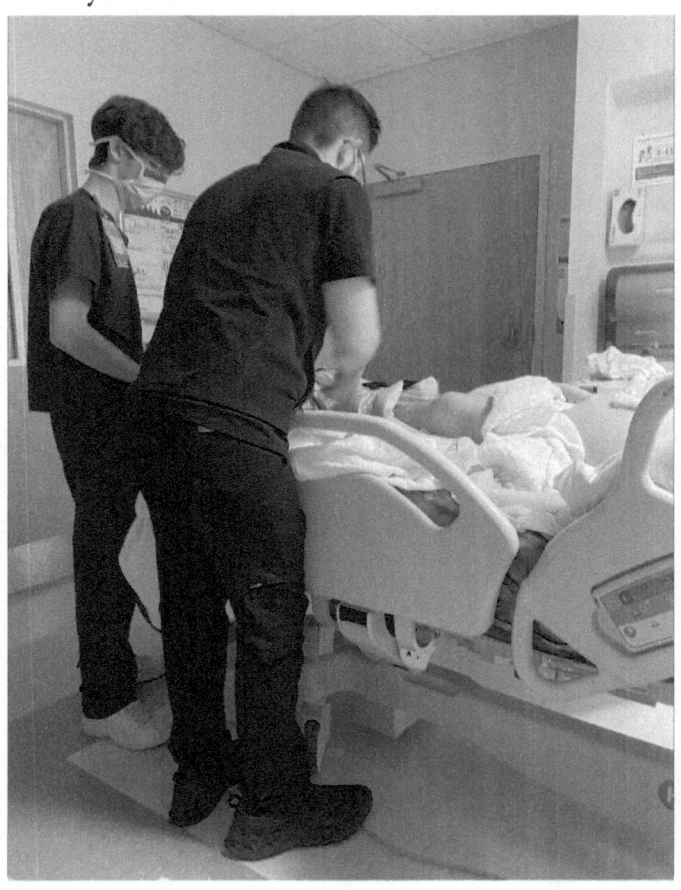

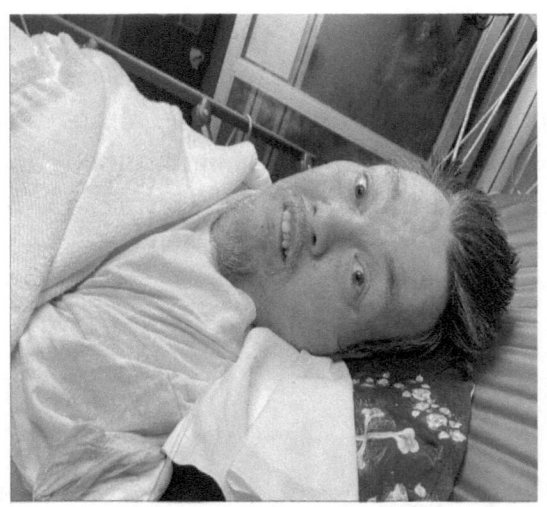

Finally, home and resting in his own bed in the same room with his big brother. It was a wonderful occasion although there were continued issues to be resolved.

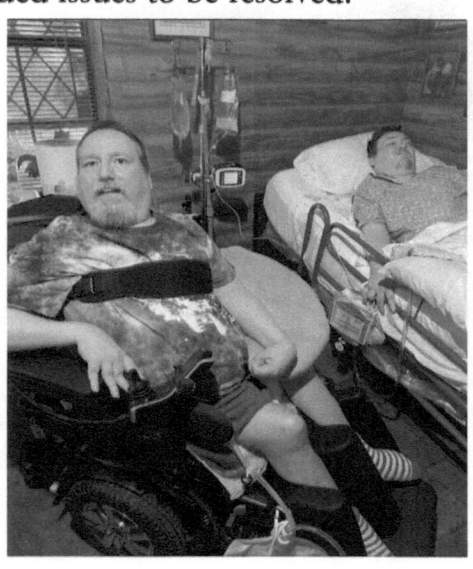

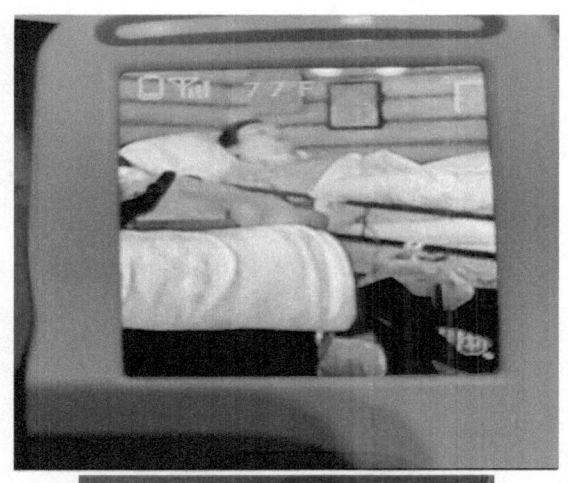

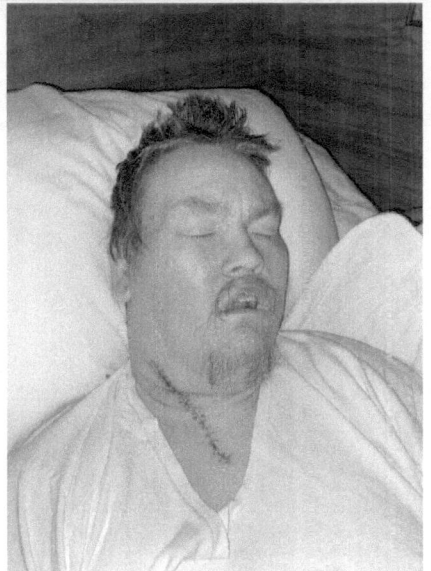

He's resting peacefully. The scare breaks our heart. But he's home.

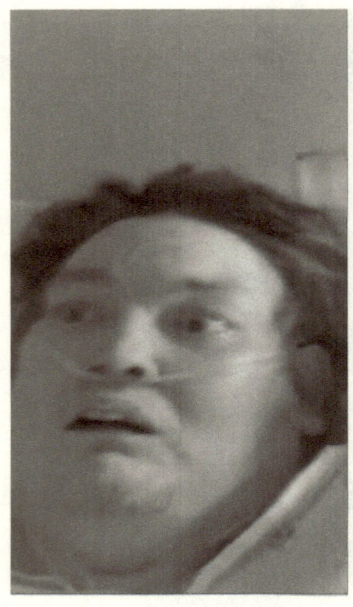

Romans 8:26

King James Version

26 Likewise the Spirit also helpeth our infirmities: for we know not what we should pray for as we ought: but the Spirit itself maketh intercession for us with groanings which cannot be uttered.

The struggle continued as Jason had embedded kidneys stones. He was still too weak for surgery to remove them. Some bladder stones were blasted apart and removed. The large stone embedded into his kidney could only be removed by surgery.

South Central Regional Medical Center ICU

He was again hospitalized with a fever of 106. The sepsis had returned.

The following pictures were taken of our Jaybird after he was resuscitated. He didn't have to be intubated but for a few hours. When he regained consciousness, he was saying Jesus. That was his only word for days. It's no doubt in our minds that he saw Jesus. His nurses were wonderful. They were stationed between only 2 patients where they could monitor them closely. That was the key to saving Jason's life. SCRMC ICU and staff are amazing.

He heard my voice.

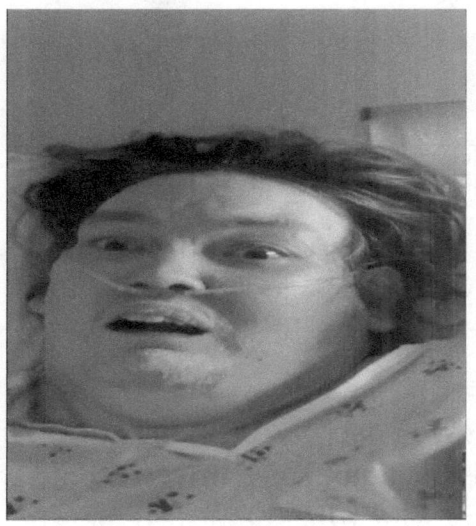

Jason was hospitalized in November 201 at Wayne General Hospital with a fever. He was transferred from Wayne Hospital General Hospital to Rush Hospital in Meridian with sepsis.

Jason spent Christmas 2021 in the hospital. A small Christmas and his presents were taken to him. And Shawn was able to visit him.

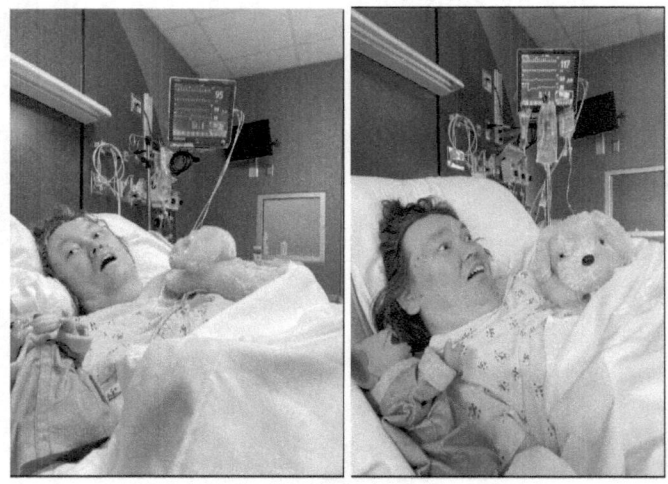

Jason came home January 2, 2022

His fever is under control. The continuing battle with sepsis and the embedded kidney stone remained a major issue. We continued praying.

This time we put balloons at the driveway because the ambulance drivers would miss the driveway. One time they called me, and I could hear Jason laughing in the background because he knew they had missed the driveway. He had himself a joy ride!!! The EMTs were wonderful.

The EMTs handled Jason with tenderness and care

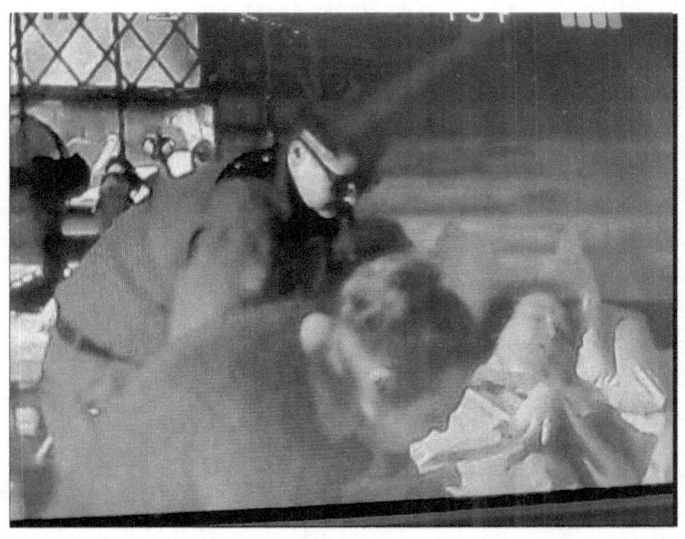

Jason would be fever free for 5 months. Every day we praised God. But he never got stable enough to have the large staghorn stone removed from his kidney. He had a pressure sore on his buttocks which wouldn't heal. We would get it better than he'd be hospitalized and come home with it worse.

He was again taken to Wayne General Hospital in June 2022 and spent his birthday in the hospital. The nurses were so sweet they gave him a haircut. He had pneumonia. He came home July 1, 2022. His fever spiked again, and he was hospitalized again. He was getting weaker. Many prayers were sent up. He now had double pneumonia. The ambulance brought him home on 7/13/2022 with a fever and no order for oxygen. The doctor was called. He was readmitted into ICU the night of 7/13/2022. Jason gained his wings at 10:30 am 7/14/2022. Holding his hand as I watched the monitor flat line for the third time and saying No more took the life out of me. My baby boy has gone home. His heavenly home where he was fully healed. No more pain. No more wheelchair. He was free but dear God it hurt. Oh, dear Lord, how will I tell Shawn. As I returned home, I was preparing to tell Shawn. I entered the house as I looked at Shawn, I could tell he knew. Tears in his eyes I hugged him without saying anything. None were needed.

The days ahead were blurry and tearful. We tried to keep a regular schedule for Shawn. I slept in Jason's bed in the room with Shawn. He barely talked. Our minister Mark Covington, who had been with us through the hardship of Jason's illness and passing, talked with Shawn. One day as we were all sitting on the front porch something happened. Laney first spoke saying "did you hear that." Mark replied, "Yes a voice whispered Kathy, everything is going to be alright." Everyone heard it but me. I was focusing on Shawn. I saw his reaction. Three days later Shawn joined his brother.

July 29, 2022

There was no warning. No health problems were noticed all day. We said our prayers and went to bed. I woke up the next morning and couldn't wake Shawn up. He was gone. Doctors said it was a blood clot. We all knew he couldn't stay without his brother. What did I miss? What could I have done differently? I would run this through my mind forever and still do. How could this be??!! I was devastated unable to make a full sentence for 3 months. Planning a celebration of life for them was delayed. I couldn't walk or talk. I couldn't eat. I often asked if I could go home too. My purpose here was finished in my mind as my sons were fully healed and safe in the arms of Jesus. Mark was a constant. He stayed with me for several days. Laney had Covid and quarantined. Tammy came and stayed to help. My life purpose was completed. I didn't know what to do anymore. My reason for living was gone.

Compare Butterflies and Souls
by Kathy Yvonne Pounds Graham

Stage one: As humans we begin as an egg inside the mother. As the egg is fertilized it begins the second stage of development. At this point all we do is feed from the mother and sleep. It takes about 9 months at which time a human is born. Stage three: From birth we are robbed of a fleshy cocoon. At first, we must be fed all the time to grow to maturity! As we mature our fleshly cocoon grows. And yes! We shed parts of our skin daily! Inside this fleshly cocoon is a soul maturing and developing. As time passes, for some it may be days for others it could be decades, the soul develops and it's time for the cocoon to release the beautiful soul within to fly and shine!! Fourth stage: A beautiful soul is released! Death isn't the end!

CHAPTER 5
TESTIMONIALS

To Know Me is To Love Me.
The Heart of a Caregiver

by Helene (Laney) Lindsey

I reminisce tonight laying on bed in my bedroom tonight and wake up praying to God every morning and every night before I go to sleep how thankful and blessed, I am to be in Shawn and Jason's home. I live here now and thinking back to when I was a young woman, I had a calling from God not yet knowing to myself yet what maybe or how. My name is Helene A. Lindsey AKA Laney and would be called one of many different names through my love for them. I was a caregiver for Shawn and Jason Odle starting somewhere after 2010. To bring you where I am now let's start with my first introduction of meeting Shawn and Jason.

To begin with I was a Certified Nurse Assistant and working for their mom Kathy a separate project that Shawn and Jason were a part of for independent living. I was introduced to Shawn and Jason at the beginning but did not work with them directly until months later. You see I had ventured over to their home in the town of Waynesboro, MS as instructed and the nurse who at that time was attending to them led me into the living room where the guys sat in their wheelchairs side by side. Jason immediately got my attention and Shawn followed behind him with long extensions of their arms and me putting both of my arms out and grasping their hands in mine with a small conversation and a smile. After their warm greeting I was run through their home by the nurse attendant and spoke to me about their daily care. Their smile won my heart over, but I wasn't sure if I was capable to handle their specific needs. I was just not comfortable with the nurse's explanations and left feeling overwhelmed or was she left feeling somewhat intimidated with me about her job or what? Nevertheless, it took some time to get to know them, but Shawn and Jason touched my heart and soon after I was to become an assistant joining other caregiver to take care of our guys is how they become called.

Shawn enjoyed most of his mornings watching the morning news on tv upon waking up quiet and you could always feel the warmth in his smile. Jason was hands on ready to always talk and wanting your attention. So, he was always given one of his gadgets to hold because first and foremost if you didn't, secondly you never knew when he would have his booty in a wad. The only one object never put in his hands was the remote control to bed. So many buttons just made Jason more curious for you see Shawn's hollering immediately needed attention because Jason would have the head and foot of the bed raised up together leaving Jason only laughing to himself and in a pickle. It's the little tools that were given that helped to alert hearing them and doing health wise every minute. More importantly, keeping each other occupied when attention was given to the other during morning care.

Both were strong willed men, but I learned they had different temperaments. Shawn would always reach over and whisper to Jason words into his ears and for years I never could figure out exactly what it was that would absolutely throw Jason over the roof top. Jason would scream, holding up his arm and shaking a fist at his brother. You see there were chores to be done for part of their care, so just like morning care with each other, attention on the other was not given at the time was not always seen but heard. In the heat of their argument, I now was to become the sheriff, don't want to be was the time to let them rectify their own behaviors. And they did because they knew to each other this was wrong. After apologies to each other Shawn still got his way only because when he didn't want his brother watching tv with him Jason would occupy himself with just as he was with hands on. Whether it was listening to music one of his favorite past times was busy himself looking at a book and turning each page carefully was looking at a special book their Aunt Valerie gave both of them from a special event. This book meant the world to them and they both could look at all the places in the United States they traveled and been with their mom as advocates they were at the time.

Shawn and Jason were characters, and they loved to throw themselves into the moments on TV that were especially funny to them. Shawn wakes up one morning and bellows out, "Lucy I'm home" from the sitcom, I love Lucy show. Okay, so who's Fred? Jason of course so I followed Lucy. For weeks this went on pretending to be these characters until one doctor's appointment came up. Upon arrival at the South Central clinic in Laurel, Mississippi to see his physician Dr. Norton eagerly strolls up to the front desk to check in and the nurse asked him for his name. Shawn took a deep breath as his mom always instructed him to do before speaking, replied Ricky Riccardo. I quickly whispered out real name twice and everyone including Jason, right behind him, busted out with humor. Shawn just put on his charm and turned his wheels around with Jason to the waiting room with a smile that would melt your heart. Both guys always turned the charm on with the nurses and flirt wherever they encountered pretty women. There were other television moments they both loved called The Nanny. Watching one segment in particular with them close by with the little girl on the show and her nanny by her side singing repeatedly, I jumped in singing, anything you can do I can do better. Shawn hollers out no you can't and after Jason hearing him comes back slowly with a smirk on his face, yes, I can

Hilarious and surprising these characters were. Whether it was Watching tv or numerous visits to the Dr at specific clinics with gadgets in hand, or flirtatious ways with nurses these young me were Hilarious and surprising no matter what situation always had a way to make others happy and laugh in the heat of a day-to-day moment.

Both Shawn and Jason engaged themselves lovingly with decorations during the holidays, birthdays were special, Mother's Day, or any upcoming events through arts and crafts. These guys had their way of decorating and instead of buying it already made. Halloween was approaching along with a Halloween party planned. After their morning routine was completed and placed in their wheelchairs, rolled themselves out and headed to the TV. Brakes were placed, stopped dead in their tracks where 2 big pumpkins sat on their kitchen counter. Every counter and sink in their home were wheelchair accessible, so it wasn't hard for them to miss anything within their reach. Eyebrows raised with bulging eyes on Shawn's face and Jason's arms stretched out as if he wanted to hug this big ole pumpkin. At that moment I blurted out, okay guys it's pumpkin carving time. With a table already placed on the porch they put the pumpkins in their laps with assistance happily they rolled up to their table side by side and set them on the table. Their big white plastic hair-cutting time apron was to be used for the messy ingredients inside the pumpkin to prevent even a greater mess. With a magic marker, they drew the faces that they wanted it to look like first then carefully with assistance used a knife to cut the top of the pumpkin head off first. Now the fun begins. Assuming they had accomplished their task a long-stemmed spoon was placed in their hands after the top of the pumpkin was carved out and placed on the side of the table all contents had to be dug out. When I placed each of the pumpkins in each in each of their laps they looked like two stunned emojis saying what do I do next. Dig in without my assistance is what I replied. After a little snicker from myself, their facial expressions curled up as if smelling something nasty. The spoon in their hands didn't work so well so I insisted that they use their hands and after some relentless hesitation from them, the digging began. Watching the feeling of squish from the inside of the pumpkin contents between their fingers and the smiles on their faces these guys were experiencing fun and were allowed to make a dirty mess without feeling guilty. Mission accomplished and Shawn looked up at me and after a deep breath with an old ear-to-ear smile hollered out beam me up Scotty. The eyes nose and mouth were carved out and completed. Proud, pride, and joy sit in their laps. Let the party begin.

Meeting and greeting anyone were never a problem in their vocabulary. But over time Shawn and Jason always had curiosities about the people that entered in and out of their lives over a period. Like Mr. Eddie, my husband. Time went on and mostly during their morning care when they learned the most about me and Mr. Eddie. If I messed up and didn't do something right Shawn would in a serious voice holler out, HEY YO EDDIE. All I could do was look at him and shake my head. Then there was Jason. Jason was strong as they both were physically in a sense but, there were times when in that same sense times became a little bit reluctant only because of a little bit of laziness. I believe on his part. So, encouraging him through Mr. Eddie and letting him learn more about the person in my life I told him how much he liked French fries. So every time I needed both guys not just Jason's assistance during their morning care to grab the bars to turn to their sides, I often would tell them to let's make Mr. Eddie French fries. This particular ritual of encouragement continued for some months until one morning Jason heard let's make Mr. Eddie French fries stopped me in my tracks when Jason then grabbed the bars on the side of the bed in exhaustion turned his head to look at me and said, piss on Mr. Eddie's French fries. Laughing out loud, well that won't work no more.

However, over another period and special events, the guys got to meet Mr. Eddie. Their step-dad Rusty loved to play bluegrass music which they so much loved along with gospel music and miss him dearly since his passing. It was Shawn's birthday and both got the biggest surprise coming on that day, met Mr. Eddie for the first time. The biggest surprise of all was when Mr. Eddie pulled out his guitar and their mom and everyone sang Happy Birthday to him. From then on, their heart became an unbreakable friendship. There were many gatherings and to no great surprise no matter if it was a visit or a kind word spoken, they were always gracious and kind to others and never forgot anyone they met.

Weather permitting outings in their wheelchair with their pets Shawn's pet dog Precious and Jason's pet dog Coalee on their laps became their favorite pastime.

Freedom to drive and ride in their wheelchairs was still being cautious of the outside elements. During nice weather, the rides started with a long roll on a dirt road to the top of the hill where highway 84 runs east and west. Both Shawn and Jason waited patiently till they spotted a big truck. Once they heard the sound of a big roaring coming before a trucker spotted them, they would put their arms up clenched fist clenched as if they were reaching to toot a horn The passing trucker spotted them and would lay on the horn back at them. This particular ritual was never a dull moment for them they were always excited at the given moment and never defeated if they were teased back.

The next stroll was a stop by Mom's house on the same property. Shawn and Jason couldn't resist slipping past Mom without her knowing what they were up to. Going to visit Jazz's pen just passed mom's house was exactly what they were up to. Mom always stepped out to accompany them up to the protected fence surrounding Jazz. And, as always, Jazz was sure to welcome Shawn and Jason as well by stretching her long neck over the fence to welcome her friends approaching as well. There was sure to be a kiss on the cheek first is what Shawn encountered that tickled both guys and many snacks with horse feed from their hands which spoiled Jazz as well. Shawn and Jason always had the privilege and great respect for nature I must say.

Life for Shawn and Jason was not always perfect every day. There were days when they didn't feel well. So adjustments for their day just need a simple solution. If meant spending the day in bed for either one of them brother never left brother's side. Jason spent more time in bed along with more and frequent stays in the hospital. Shawn's concerns for his brother and having to not being able to have him by his side for days or weeks yes worried him. So the use of technology lessened his concerns by using video calling. Talking directly on the phone and if Jason was close by he was driven to the hospital Shawn always felt he was right by his side along with many prayers prayed. Every time Jason returned home from his hospital stays. Shawn would shed tears of joy upon his return. This went on for about the last 2 years of Jason's life here on earth. Life for them was changing for each other but no matter what the circumstances were they never changed. They adapted and accepted what had come to them by the grace of God and protected each other. By the year 2022 staying positive and hopeful became the year where Shawn and Jason accepted in their hearts, love and loss were coming. The new loss, the new grief and they felt the loss of others that surrounded them. My husband and their friend Mr. Eddie passed away after a short period of illness passed away on June 3rd, 2022. But faith remained hopeful in all our hearts.

I share with you since many seasons have

come and gone as have Shawn and Jason now. They lived a defined life for others. They share a legacy for others which is you can't ever let others tell you that you can't do anything. You just need to do things differently. The stories of their lives simplifies life, love, and the pursuit of happiness. We all here and around the world share one thing in common: What an almighty God we serve. Through others and God, all things are possible.

Goodnight Shawn I love you and Jason whispered to me in a loving voice You love me too? You bet I do love you and brother too. Both of you always .

Caregivers
Tammy Hoggle

There was a time in my life I was going through so many battles I was living with my mom at the time and I started dating this guy he told me the personality I had I could be a caretaker I told him I had never done anything like that except take care of my mom but I would try so he took me to Waynesboro Mississippi and I met Kathy, Jason (aka JayBird) and Shawn (aka Stinker) Thats what I called them.

Those 2 young men were my miracle because they put so much joy, laughter and love into my life. No matter what I was going through in my life I always found joy and peace around them.

When I was around those two working and caring for them, it seemed like I was playing with them. I didn't want to leave at the end of my shift.

When I first started I was scared to death but that quickly disappeared. Shawn (Stinker) took a while to get close to me. He watched everything I did. But Jason (JayBird) had me wrapped around his finger from Day 1. He was very outgoing and carefree. He was very generous with his love and praises.

Once I got relaxed and they both got close to me emotionally they touched my heart every day. It was like God telling me I was where I was supposed to be. When they passed it was devastating to all of us. More devastating was watching their mother grieve fearing we would lose her too. when those 3 were together you could feel nothing but love and peace.

My favorite game with them was Stinker would tell me he was calling the 'po po' police on me. I'd get the blue Nerf gun with the red balls and say 'Go ahead I'm ready' as I was shooting the red balls up toward the ceiling. They would laugh. Then they would chase me around the bar island in the kitchen in their wheelchairs.

They loved their snack time. They would get ice cream and sometimes mom's banana pudding.

We sing songs.

Sundays were totally set aside for worshipping and praising God. They enjoyed church services in their room listening to preaching. Those are some of the special times shared with those two. I will never forget and shall forever cherish these memories.

I truly admire Kathy and the way she looked out for them. It's amazing how she kept them involved in all she did. She always took them with her whenever possible so they got to see many wonderful places. They touched so many lives in so many ways. They proved with God anything is possible.

Tammie Brown Personal care attendant

Cheering on our favorite football team. It didn't matter who won it was a memory I will never forget with Shawn.

My Birthday cookie cake from Shawn and Jason. Of course I was gonna let them have some icing.

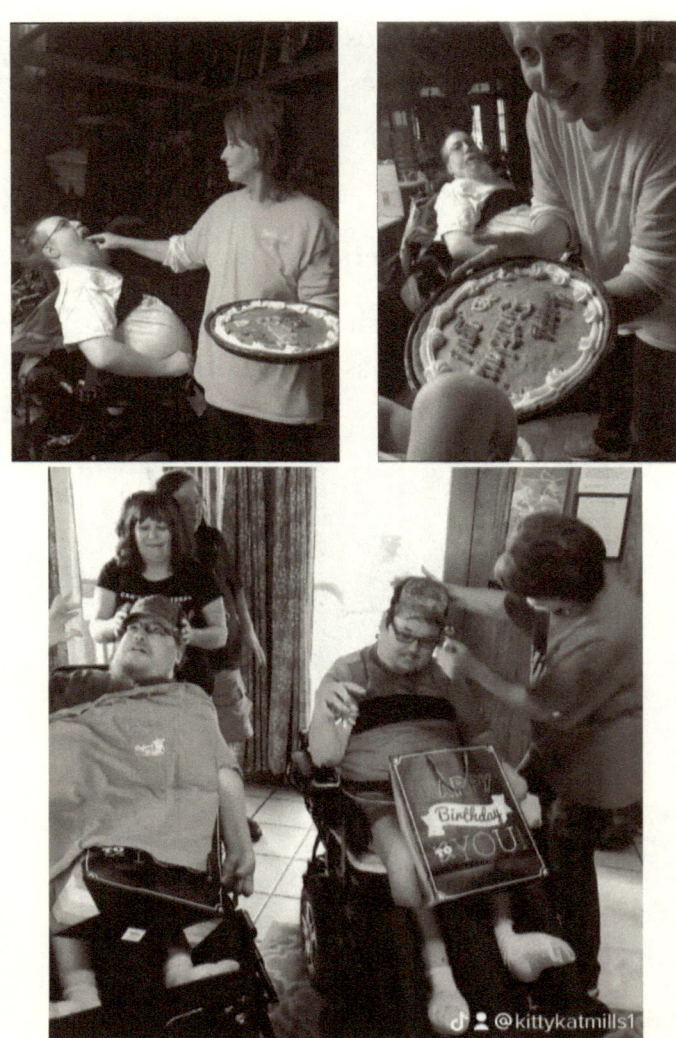

Birthday celebrations with these two was the best. I miss them days. They were so excited and the laughter from them said it all.

I wish I could go back to this day with them. It was all about them and I wouldn't trade anything for this day I spent with them. Love and miss them more than anything.

By Minister Mark Covington:

I had the privilege of coming into their lives when they were but teenagers. These brothers made me a better Minister and a better man. I will always remember them as men of great faith, great hope, and great love.

Connie H Brewer, RN

I had the pleasure of meeting Kathy and her sons several years ago. She has dedicated herself totally to her boys. I sat with them for a couple of months at night. They were always happy. They loved each other and their mama. They were blessings from the Lord and they were blessed to have their mama. It was a privilege getting to be a part of this family.

Marian Allen, BA, MSW, LMSW
COMMUNITY SERVICES CASE MANAGER

I am writing to share my heartfelt testimony regarding my experiences working with Shawn and Jason Odle, two brothers born with Pelizaeus-Merzbacher disease, a rare genetic disorder. Their lives were a testament to love and perseverance. Working with individuals with disabilities particularly those who may not communicate verbally but express themselves through their smiles and other nonverbal cues. Throughout my time as their social worker, I had the privilege of interacting with remarkable individuals. Each home visit reinforced the belief that communication transcends words. Those smiles of Shawn and Jason conveyed emotions, stories, and connections that some words fail to express. Whether it was a gentle grin, unexcited laugh, or a serene expression every smile was a testament to their unique perspective and experience.

They taught me to be more attuned to non-verbal signals. These interactions have not only enriched my understanding of empathy but also deepened my appreciation for the diverse ways in which people communicate and connect.

Submitted by Vicki Killingsworth

Kathy, Shawn, and Jason are some of the most courageous and determined people I have ever met. Kathy was determined to give her boys the opportunities they're able-bodied peers had and some took for granted. All three of them had the courage to face the No's that seem to be around every corner of progress and Independence for them. Kathy did not accept no for an answer she went a step further and taught people how to turn the no into yes. With her southern belle charm and determination. Kathy and her boys opened many doors for people with disabilities across the country. Not only did she have to force some of those doors open but she did it with style and grace. When I met Kathy she already had so many things put in place and ready to go for her sons. She had a trust fund set up and all the people necessary to continue allowing Jason and Shawn to live independently in their own home in the event something happened to her. Shawn and Jason were two of the first people in the Home of Your Own program at the Institute for Disability Studies. A national program that assisted people with disabilities and purchasing their own homes to include all the necessary supports to live independently in their own home. Shawn and Jason both with severe disabilities bought their own home and had staff that would make sure that they were taken care of 24 hours a day. Kathy would come and go as a caregiver as well. One of my favorite memories is when Shawn and Jason truly made their independence known. Kathy was coming for a weekend with her overnight bag when barely in the door the boys said, " You're not moving back in are you? "or was it "You aren't moving back in." I suspect it was the first one but regardless it was definitely a statement of Independence that was quite clear. Many people owe these three people much gratitude for their present day Independence that would have not been possible without courage and determination of these three wonderful people.

Teacher Testimonial:

I had the pleasure of reaching both Shawn and Jason Odle who were both a challenge and a delight. The greatest pleasure and challenge came with working with their mother, Kathy. She not only advocated for them but also helped the system and their teachers in finding solutions to enhance her sons' education and social development. There was no such words as impossible nor can't be done in her book. Her sons were just as determined. I'll never forget them being taken to the principal's office for leaving skid marks in their powered wheelchairs on the hallway floor. They kept all of us on our toes. I am so glad and forever blessed to have been a part of their lives.

Mom's Testimony
My Daily Dose of Possibility Thinking
My Blessings My Sons Kathy Pounds Graham

From the day you were born until you're passing, the two of you were the joy of my life. You were and still are God's greatest blessing. The two of you made me think with a positive mind into the reality of alternative possibilities. You challenged me to think beyond the limits of society's norms and see the endless capabilities of the human mind. You showed me truly where there's the will there is a way. You brought me closer to God through spiritual growth and physical challenges. You taught me the very essence of being human: to be gentle and kind, to care, to respect, to encourage one another and to love endlessly despite the obstacles. I praise God every day for the opportunity of being your mother. I pray each day I fulfilled my role with every ounce of love and strength God gave me. Missing you is difficult. I do it every day. Loving you is easy because it never fades. I know I will see both of you again this time you will be free of all the burdens of this world. You are made whole. Thank you, Jesus, for being the sacrifice for our salvation. Thank you, Shawn and Jason, for an awesome life!!

Lovingly Forever, Mom.

CHAPTER 6
CELEBRATION OF LIVES WELL LIVED

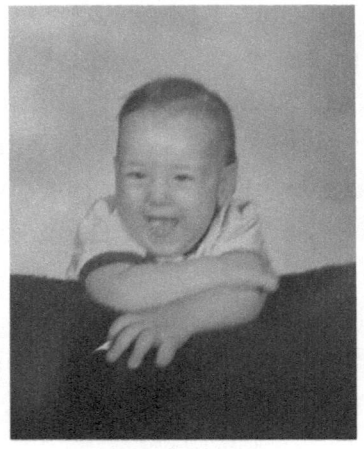

Shawn Riley Odle
10/04/1974 - 7/29/2022

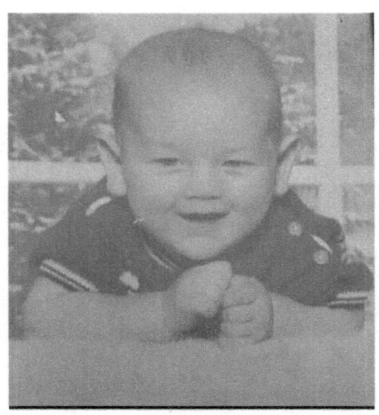

Jason Silas Odle
6/15/1977 - 7/14/2022

Brothers' love

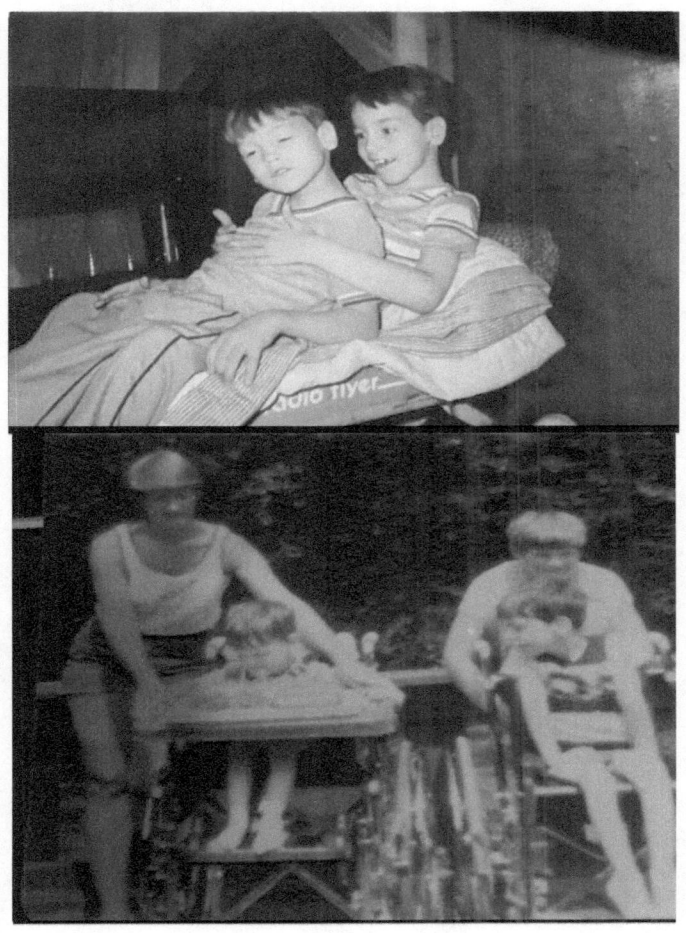

Christmas 1987

Jason slipping his dog King a cookie

Shawn's first sight of Jason. Nothing but love.

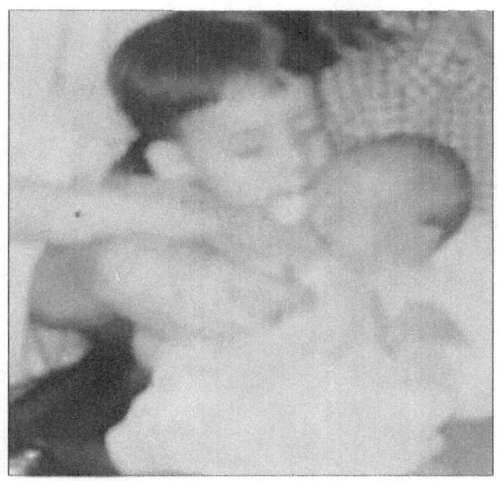

Partners in accomplishments

A love like no other the love of a mother and the love of brothers.

Partners in crime

Uncle Norman and Shawn

Shawn in first grade

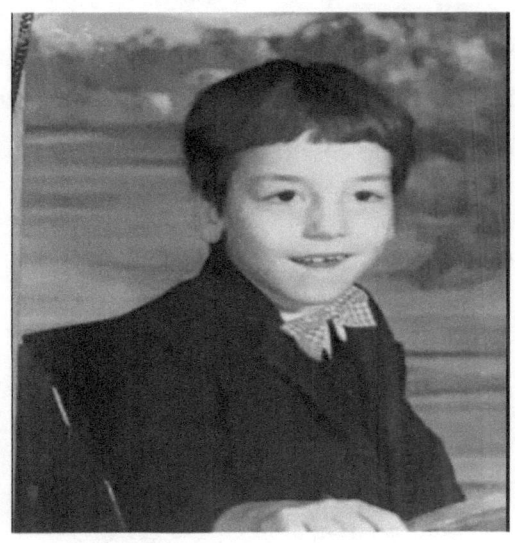

Let's go camping!!!

They enjoyed outing and going swimming.
Yes they could swim even though they had no
balance to sit stand or walk.

The love they shared for each other and others
was the purest and closest to God's love on
this earth.

My graduation from Ole Miss

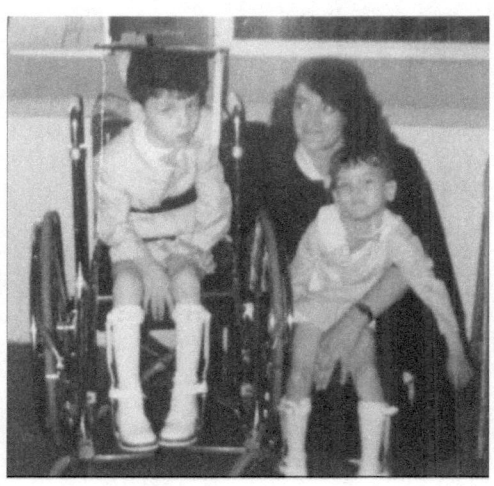

They were my reason, my motivation and purpose.

Our team in Washington DC

I never had to worry about my sons' souls but there was a constant worrying about what others could do to harm them. I am thankful for 47 years of the most wonderful love 🤍 a mother could have. I'm also thankful they are safe in His Arms now away from all harm. 🙌

In 2004 Rusty lost both legs due to diabetes. He joined our guys in the world of wheel mobilization. His statement was 'God knew what he was doing when he put y'all in my life.' The change was a hard one, but Shawn and Jason were his encouragement and motivation.

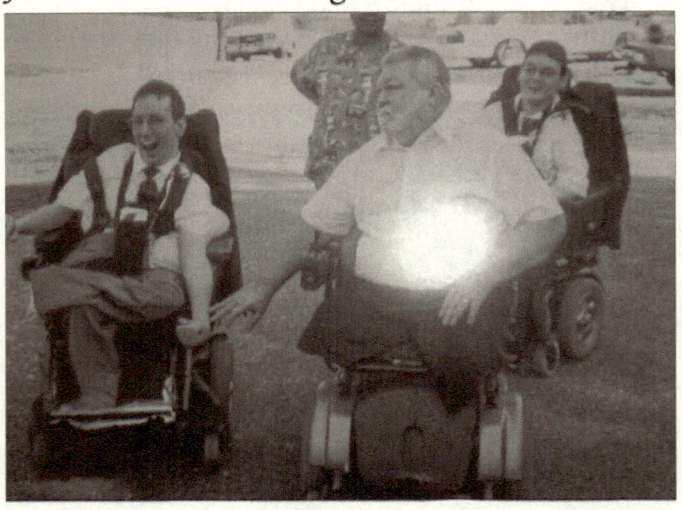

They enjoyed their male friends visiting.

Carter

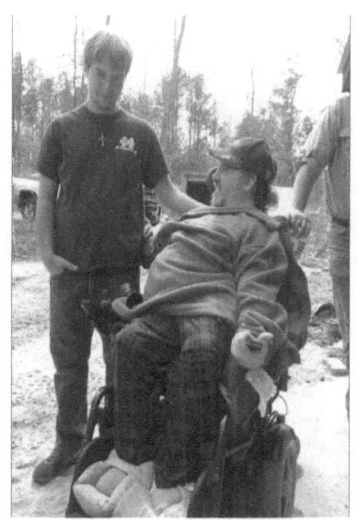

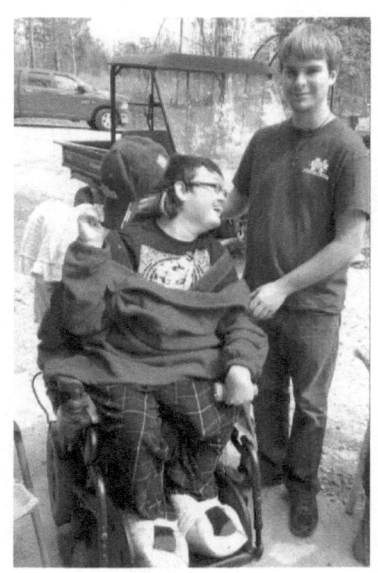

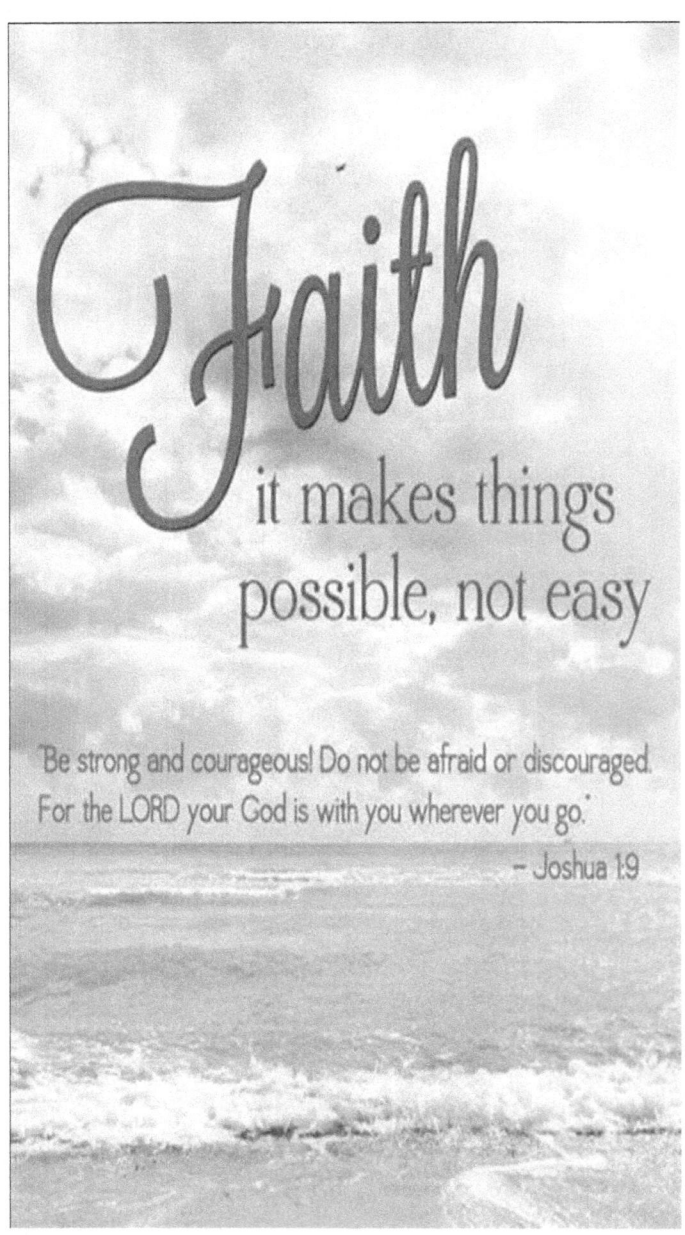

Faith

it makes things possible, not easy

"Be strong and courageous! Do not be afraid or discouraged. For the LORD your God is with you wherever you go."

– Joshua 1:9

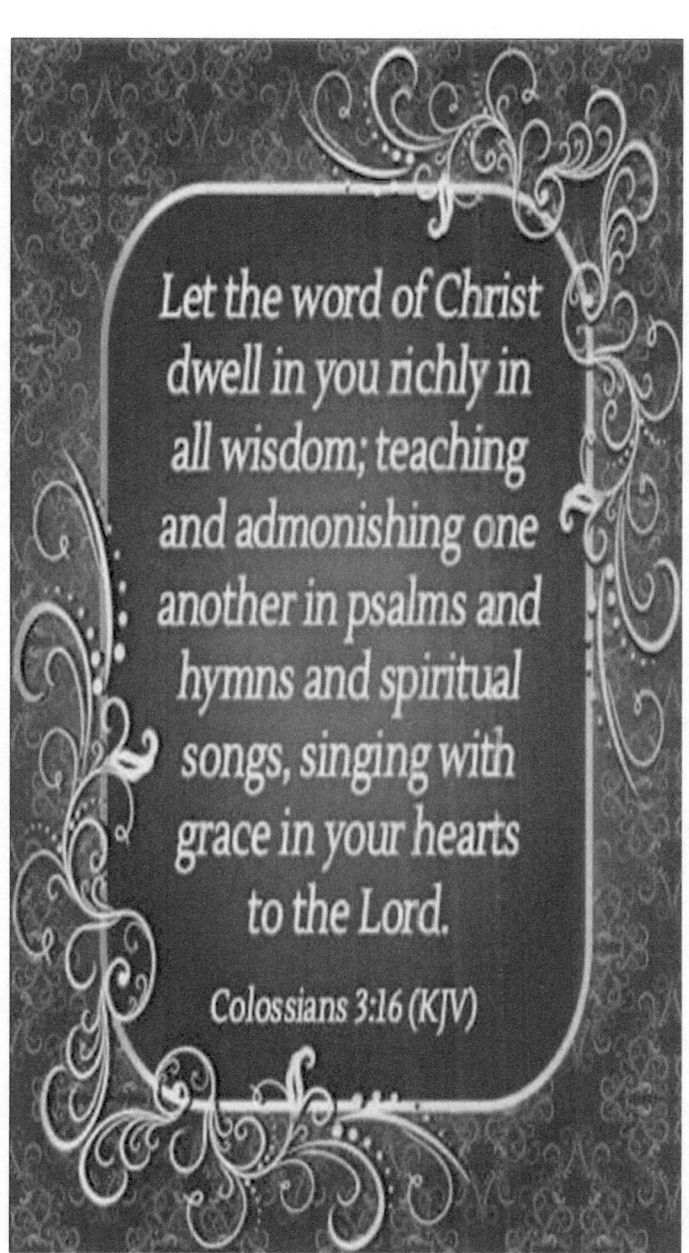

Let the word of Christ dwell in you richly in all wisdom; teaching and admonishing one another in psalms and hymns and spiritual songs, singing with grace in your hearts to the Lord.

Colossians 3:16 (KJV)

Bill came to see Jason on Christmas in the hospital in 2019.

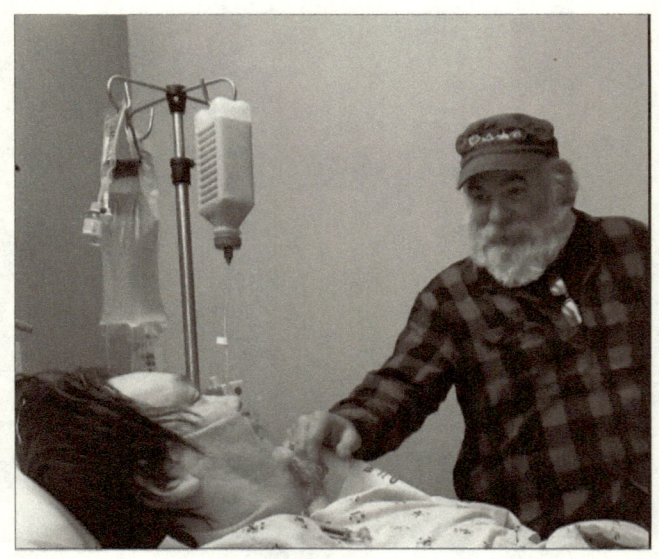

This was a hot summer day when Bill Harvison was laying a stone around their log home. As he finished on the south side Shawn had his back turned. Bill wet him with the water hose. Words came from Shawn's mouth none of us had ever heard him say and you could forget about him apologizing. Jason was bursting a button laughing. Thank you, Bill!!

Rusty and Grandma Mildred at their first
home warming

Shawn's birthday and Eddie and Laney's renewal of vows. A confererate wedding

DSid came to visit from Texas

Jason loved his cuddling with mom.

Their ministry GOAL

Always smiling. Always happy.

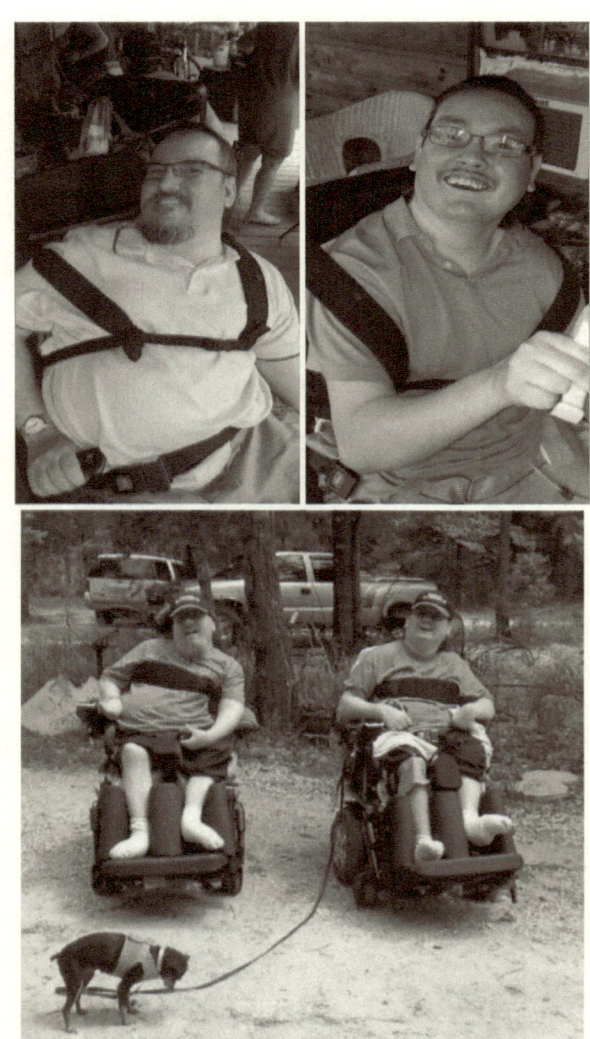

Finishing high school

A Celebration of Life ceremony was held on the place they loved SeldoMResT FarM at FoxFire in Wayne County, Mississippi. Attendees were given the opportunity to give testimony to their lives. Videos were made. There were several occurrences which showed the angels presence with them. Such is the picture below.

Following the ceremony dove balloons were released with their pictures on them. So unexpectedly one of Jason's balloons ns went hopping and bouncing up the east driveway before taking flight. That was so typical of his nature. We named that driveway JayBird Drive. The west driveway was named Shawn's Way.

Love connection forever

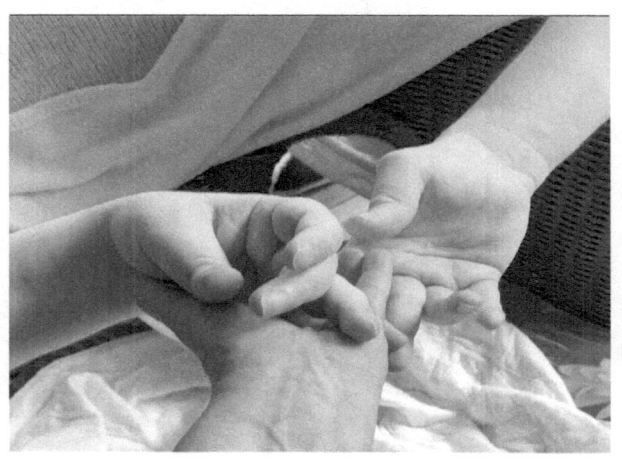

Philippians 4:6-7

⁴Always be full of joy in the Lord. I say it again—rejoice! ⁵Let everyone see that you are considerate in all you do. Remember, the Lord is coming soon.

⁶Don't worry about anything; instead, pray about everything. Tell God what you need, and thank him for all he has done. ⁷Then you will experience God's ᵏpeace, which exceeds anything we can understand. His peace will guard your hearts and minds as you live in Christ Jesus.

⁸And now, dear brothers and sisters, one final thing. Fix your thoughts on what is true, and honorable, and right, and pure, and lovely, and admirable. Think about

The days you miss them more, hurt deeper, or struggle to breathe—
I don't call them bad days.

Nothing born from the love I hold for them could ever be bad.
Heavy, yes. But not bad.
It's God's love in its purest form.

Written for Their Celebration of Life Memorial by their uncle , my brother in law Daniel Buchanan, Minister at the Great Falls Church of Christ.

Letter from Shawn and Jason

To All, Especially Mama,

We are sending you this letter today, on the wings of a snow-white dove. We know you have heard of our passing from this earth and have shed many tears for us.

Please, my dear loved ones, cry for us no more. Or at least, cry no tears of pain. If you must cry, let them be tears of joy, for we are finally free.

There is no more pain. No more wheelchair. No more frustration. The days when our voices were trapped in our minds are gone.

When we took our last breath on Earth, we were not alone. Jesus held our hands as we closed our eyes for the last time. He lifted us up to Heaven, where so many wonderful, loved ones were waiting to greet us with joy.

This thing you call death has liberated us. Ha! You didn't know we knew that word, did you?

We are disencumbered, unimpeded, emancipated, and free. Yes, we know all these words; we just couldn't express them. Now we can express ourselves with so many words.

We can walk and even run everywhere we go. There is no need for our wheelchair anymore, and we truly do love to run. (Don't tell Jason, but I, Shawn, am faster!)

We are even singing with the angels. And though we will never sing as beautifully as they do, we have to say that we don't sound half bad. (Don't tell Shawn, but I, Jason, sing better than him!)

It is so beautiful here. There is no pain. The only tears are tears of joy. Mama, don't you fear. We will always be there with you. Look for us in the blooms of sweet flowers. Look for us in the billowing clouds in the sky; we will draw you a picture with our new fingers in them. Look for us, in the sunset; we will paint you the most beautiful sunset. Look for us in the warm breeze; we will kiss your cheeks with our new lips.

Sometimes, just for the fun of it, just to make you laugh, we will send a shower of rain upon your head on the brightest, sunshine-filled day. You will know it is just for you from us, and we expect you to laugh and dance in the rain with us.

Mama, we have always loved you and will always love you.

LOVE ALWAYS, Shawn and Jason

Today I am able to accomplish the completion of their books Hearts of Gold Broken Bodies. It has taken mountains of strength and tons of tears to release their story to the world. It is with a humble heart and praises to God that I submit my sons' story and life accomplishments to the world. I pray it encourages those who encounter life challenges. I hope it widens the understanding of the world to the possibilities of the normal impossibilities in the human mind. I pray it brings normalization through representation of their lives and others like them.

My command is this: Love each other as I have loved you."
— John 15:12